THE ANCIENT CHINESE

Julia Waterlow

Look into the Past

The Ancient Chinese
The Ancient Japanese
The Anglo-Saxons
The Aztecs
The Egyptians
The Greeks
The Incas
The Maya
The Normans
The Romans
The Sioux
The Tudors & Stuarts
The Victorians
The Vikings

Series editor: Joanna Bentley
Series designer: David West
Book designer: Joyce Chester

First published in 1994 by Wayland (Publishers) Ltd,
61 Western Road, Hove, East Sussex, BN3 1JD, England.

© Copyright 1994 Wayland (Publishers) Ltd

British Library Cataloguing in Publication Data
Waterlow, Julia
    Ancient Chinese. – (Look into the Past
    Series)
    I. Title II. Series
    931

ISBN 0 7502 1067 2

Typeset by Dorchester Typesetting Group Ltd., Dorset,
England.
Printed and bound in Italy by L.E.G.O. S.p.A., Vicenza,
Italy.

Picture acknowledgements

The publishers wish to thank the following for providing the
photographs in this book: E.T. Archive cover, 7 (top,
Bibliothèque Nationale, Paris; bottom, National Palace
Museum, Taiwan), 9 (both, Freer Gallery of Art,
Washington, USA), 12 (National Palace Museum, Taiwan),
15 (bottom), 17 (right, British Museum), 19 (top, British
Library; bottom, Bibliothèque Nationale, Paris), 21 (top,
National Palace Museum, Taiwan), 23 (top, National Palace
Museum, Taiwan), 27 (top, Bibliothèque Nationale, Paris);
Werner Forman Archive 10 (Peking Palace Museum), 13
(right, Metropolitan Museum, New York), 16 (Shaanxi
Provincial Museum, Xian), 20 (right, Idemitsu Museum,
Tokyo), 25 (top), 27 (bottom, Peking Palace Museum);
Robert Harding cover, 15 (top, Freer Gallery of Art), 24, 25
(bottom), 29 (top, courtesy Museum of Fine Arts, Boston,
USA); Michael Holford cover, 23; The Needham Research
Institute 22; Julia Waterlow cover, 5 (both), 6, 8 (both), 11
(both), 13 (top), 14, 17 (left), 20 (left), 21 (bottom), 26, 28,
29 (bottom).
Artwork on page 4 by Stephen Wheele; page 18 by Julia
Waterlow.

CONTENTS

Words that appear in ***bold italic*** in the text are explained in the glossary on page 30.

THE MIDDLE KINGDOM

Stretching back at least 5,000 years, China's *civilization* has lasted without a break to this day. For many Chinese, life now is much as it would have been hundreds of years ago; no other country has managed to survive throughout history in this way. Unlike most other ancient societies, China kept itself very much to itself and the Chinese thought they were the most important civilization on Earth. Their own name for China – the Middle Kingdom – shows how they have always believed their country to be at the centre of the world.

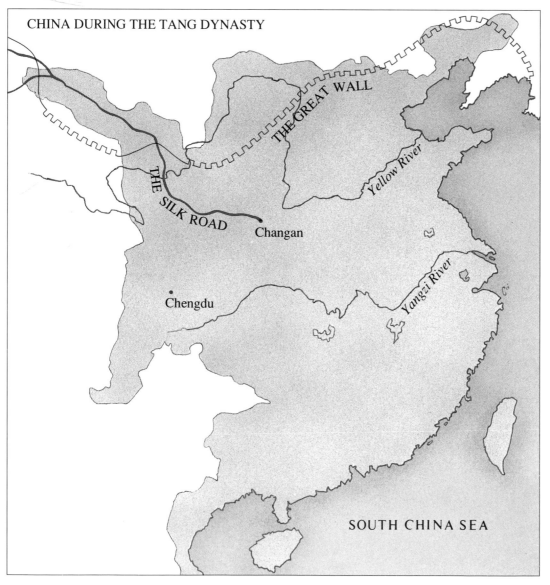

CHINA DURING THE TANG DYNASTY

THE GREAT WALL

THE SILK ROAD

Yellow River

Yangzi River

Changan

Chengdu

SOUTH CHINA SEA

◀ The heart of ancient China was the area around the Yellow River in the north, where settlements dating back to about 5000 BC have been found. In about 2000 BC the first Chinese *dynasty* was founded. Between about 800 and 200 BC the land was split into many different states, which were often at war with each other, but China was finally united into one country by the Qin emperor in 221 BC. From then on, China grew into a well-organized society, the Han (206 BC – AD 220) and Tang (AD 618 – 907) dynasties being the ones most remembered for their industry, culture and government.

▲ Most people lived in the valleys of the Yellow and Yangzi Rivers where there was usually plenty of water and crops grew well in the *fertile* soil. Mountains and deserts to the west cut China off from the rest of the world. Only a few traders, such as the Italian, Marco Polo, braved the long and hard overland journey. As a result of being so remote, the Chinese have always been *self-sufficient*. This is the scenery around part of the Yellow River valley. Sometimes the rains failed here in northern China and there were terrible *droughts* when thousands of people died.

◄ Hundreds of people are working to mend the banks of the Yellow River to stop it flooding. Although the Yellow River provided much-needed water, it also often flooded. A *legend* tells how Minister Yu, who struggled for years trying to stop the Yellow River floods, was made emperor of the first ever Chinese dynasty because his work was so important. Throughout history, emperors have used the huge numbers of people in China to work on large projects like building walls and canals.

THE RULERS OF CHINA

China was ruled by emperors. Most came from a long line of people from the same family, called a dynasty. This *imperial* system lasted even until early this century. The emperor was believed to be the son of heaven and was treated as a god. When there were uprisings or terrible natural disasters such as earthquakes, it was thought that heaven was angry and the dynasty would fall.

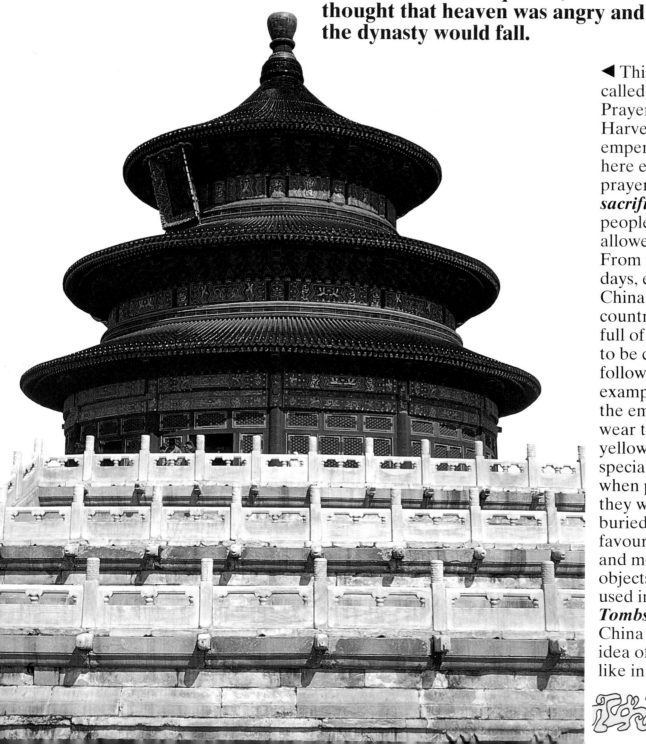

◄ This temple is called the Hall of Prayer for Good Harvests. The emperor used to come here every year to say prayers and make *sacrifices*. Ordinary people were not allowed to watch. From the earliest days, even before China became one country, court life was full of *rituals* that had to be carefully followed – for example, no one but the emperor could wear the colour yellow. There were special *ceremonies* when people died and they were often buried with their favourite possessions and models of useful objects that could be used in the afterlife. *Tombs* found in China give us a good idea of what life was like in those days.

◄ The Qin emperor who first united China was a strong but cruel man. The picture shows him ordering the burning of books – he wanted to destroy any ideas that were not his own, especially ideas from the past. Thousands of people were forced to work on his great projects – building roads, canals and the Great Wall. But these helped China become a strong united country, as did his laws making a common written language and *standardizing* weights and measures. He is well remembered too for his last great scheme, his tomb which was guarded by clay models of soldiers (see page 24). It is said that 700,000 people worked for 36 years to build it.

People were divided roughly into four levels in ancient Chinese society, below the emperor. There were no written laws about people's rank, but everyone knew their place. At the top was the emperor and underneath him were *scholars* and state officials like this one who is being bowed to by his visitors. The Chinese valued people who worked on the land, and so the *peasants* were considered the next most important. Below them were craftsmen and lowest of all were merchants and shopkeepers.▼

FARMING THE LAND

Farming in China began in the Yellow River valley but spread outwards as the empire grew. In the north farmers grew *millet* and wheat, but from the Yangzi River south, rice was their main crop. The south was warmer and had more rainfall. There were mulberry trees too, the leaves of which were used to feed silk-worms. *Hemp* was grown to make poor people's clothes as well as being used for fuel.

▲ Rice terraces in southern China today are built up the hillsides just as they always have been. In order to feed the large *population* every bit of land was used. People were encouraged to produce more grain than they needed so that the extra could be stored for times when the harvests were not so good, such as in times of drought or war.

◀ Peasants bring water from an irrigation channel up to the rice fields using a *treadmill*, one of the many practical inventions thought up by the ancient Chinese. By 700 BC iron was being used to make metal tools such as *ploughs* and hoes. This made farming much easier and more crops could be produced. Other inventions like the wheelbarrow were a great help in carrying things around.

◀ Farmers in China needed regular water supplies. *Irrigation* canals like this one were built during the Han dynasty to bring water even to remote border regions on the edge of the desert. The Qin emperor built a famous scheme called the Min River project. It controlled and fed water on to the rich farming area of the Chengdu plain. Today, 2,000 years later, it is still used to irrigate fields in the area.

These peasants who are planting out their rice would have to give the crop from one of their fields to the state. It was like a tax.

CITY LIFE

The cities of ancient China were large and well organized. During the Tang dynasty, the capital Changan had a population of about one million, bigger than any other city in the world at that time. Hangzhou, a city during the Song dynasty (AD 960-1279), also with over one million people, needed two hundred tonnes of rice every day to feed them all. Even though there were large cities like this, most people lived in small villages in the countryside.

This *pagoda*, ▶ called the Big Goose Pagoda, was built in AD 648 in the city of Changan. Like all Chinese cities, Changan was square in shape and surrounded by strong, high walls. These stretched over 24 kilometres and had gates that were closed at night. Inside, the streets were laid out in a grid pattern, with different areas for each class of people. Changan was so large that the buildings spread well beyond the city walls.

◀ This picture shows the bustling crowds and busy markets in the city of Kaifeng. The cities were centres for trade and people would come from all around. There were shops of every kind. The Song city of Hangzhou was said to have had seventy-two restaurants open day and night; some of them were floating restaurants on a lake. There was entertainment, from singing and theatre to drinking and gambling.

These buildings are built in the same way as those in ancient China. The houses of the wealthy were made of wood and had coloured tiled roofs. The roofs were curved to keep away evil spirits which were believed to move in straight lines: people took care to build in the right way to keep the spirits happy. Houses had walls all around with a large courtyard inside. Poorer people in the countryside had houses made of mud bricks with roofs of reeds. ▼

HOME AND FAMILY

Families in China were usually large with many generations living together. The Chinese believed that the family was very important and its good name should be continued. Most houses had an altar at which the family would regularly pray to the spirits of their dead *ancestors*. When someone died, they would be given as grand a funeral as the family could afford. Their children wore white clothing, the colour of mourning in China, for three years afterwards.

This is a rich ▶ family during the Tang dynasty praying to the saint above them for many children and great riches. Fathers were like emperors in their own houses and expected to be obeyed in everything by their children and wives. Sometimes they had second wives, called concubines. Marriages were always arranged by the parents.

▲ Here scholars are meeting in a garden for a meal. Millet cakes, wheat noodles and rice were the basic foods, but at a rich person's banquet like this they would have many different dishes, including delicacies such as bear's paw, dog or tortoise. They are probably drinking tea or wine with their meal.

Ordinary people would only be able to afford to eat vegetables with their rice, just having meat occasionally. Food was usually cooked by boiling, steaming or frying. These methods did not use up too much expensive fuel. Everyone used chopsticks to eat their food.

This robe belonged to an empress ▶
– not everyone would have had such
lovely clothes! But rich Chinese
people often had beautifully
embroidered silk gowns like this,
sweeping to the ground. Ladies
wore their hair up, decorated with
silver or gold pins and combs.
Their jewellery was made of
jade or jewels and they wore
make-up too. Peasants working
in the fields wore simple
clothes, usually baggy trousers
and a loose top.

PLEASURES AND PASTIMES

The rich in China had more time and money to spend amusing themselves than most people. Everyone, though, enjoyed festivals and the many kinds of street entertainment in the towns such as story-tellers and singers. Nobles and officials particularly liked sports such as hunting and less active pastimes such as listening to musicians playing.

Chinese opera is still performed today much as it was in ancient China. Each opera had a story that everyone knew. The singers would dress in colourful costumes and musicians played beside the stage. The operas would sometimes last for days. The stage was usually set up in the street and could be moved to another place. Music was important at the emperor's court too – one emperor had 829 talented musicians!

▲ Here, ladies of the Tang dynasty are playing a game of 'double-sixes'. Six bamboo sticks were thrown like dice and counters moved around the board. Games like this, and chess, were very popular with everyone. The Chinese enjoyed gambling and not only betted on games but also on cock-fighting and other contests.

◄ The picture on this old Chinese plate shows a spring fishing festival. The green paper dragon people are carrying represents the ruler of the waters. There were several festivals during the year, the biggest being the New Year Festival. Doorways were pasted with red strips of paper with lucky sayings on them and feasts were prepared. Towns and villages would resound to the noise of cracking fireworks and processions through the streets.

BELIEFS

China has been called the land of three religions – Confucianism, Daoism and *Buddhism*. Neither of the first two are actually religions but many Chinese came to worship the founders of these *philosophies* and built temples to them. The Chinese have never believed in only one god as people in other parts of the world do. Mixed with these three beliefs were also popular beliefs in spirits such as river gods and ancestor spirits.

Confucius was ▶ born in 551 BC at a time when China was still made up of many different states. He travelled around from court to court explaining his ideas about how people ought to live and behave. His philosophy became the most important influence on Chinese thought right up to the present day. Confucius taught that everyone should behave properly, respecting their elders and seniors and trying to act in a fair way. The family was all-important. Rulers should be chosen by ability and good conduct, not by wealth.

This statue of the Buddha was carved into the hillside during the Tang dynasty. Buddhism has always been the most popular religion in China and at one stage during the Tang dynasty even became the state religion. The Buddha taught that people should not be concerned with worldly things and should live simply. The religion came to China from India during the Han dynasty.

▲ Very little is known about this man, Lao Zi, but we know about his teachings. He is thought to have lived about the same time as Confucius. He believed in the 'dao', which means 'way' in Chinese. In order to follow the 'way', people should live in harmony with nature, letting life carry them along. Many Daoists used to live as hermits on remote hillsides. Over the centuries, Daoist ideas became mixed with popular beliefs and magic. **17**

WRITING AND EDUCATION

When the Qin emperor made China one country in 221 BC, he also brought in a change that helped China to stay united as a culture for ever afterwards – he standardized writing across the empire. Everyone could then understand each other. This helped the spread of education which was particularly important according to Confucian ideas.

Ancient Chinese	Modern Chinese	English
☉	日	sun
	羊	sheep
	馬	horse
	田	field
	水	water
	木	tree
	鳥	bird

Chinese words are not made up from letters of the alphabet but instead use a character or simplified picture for each word. Although there were some changes to Chinese writing early on, it has remained the same for hundreds of years. The earliest form of writing was on 'oracle bones and shells', animal bones and tortoise shells used to foretell the future. They date from about 1500 BC. Writing developed into an art and, using a brush, educated people would spend hours perfecting their characters into beautiful script.

18

This is a page from the oldest printed ▶
book in the world, the Diamond Sutra, a
Buddhist book dated 11 May AD 868. Paper
was invented in China in about AD 105; before
then everything was written on silk or wood.
Printing was developed in China between the
fourth and seventh centuries AD, and it meant
that many more people had a chance to read
and learn. Printing did not reach Europe until
the fifteenth century.

◀ Here scholars are
taking examinations
to become officials in
the government. It
could take years to
pass all the necessary
tests. Only
rich and important
men were able to take
part – the poor had no
education at all. Boys
from the upper classes
would start studying
at about the age of
ten, having to learn
works by Confucius
off by heart. An
educated person was
supposed to be
talented in other ways
too, such as being a
good musician or
painter.

CREATIVE CHINA

Over 5,000 years ago the Chinese started making decorative pots and the early dynasties worked bronze to create elegant dishes and bowls. Most were made for ceremonies and rituals. From the time of the Han dynasty, art began to be enjoyed for its own sake and in later dynasties painting, music and poetry were studied by most educated people in China.

The Chinese started using a wheel to make pottery in about 2000 BC. They then discovered a fine white clay that could be used to make porcelain (also called china in the rest of the world because it first came from China). Large potteries were set up near where the clay was found and beautiful fine china was made. Both these pieces of pottery were made in the Tang dynasty.

◀ This picture was painted during the Song dynasty and shows a Tang dynasty emperor fleeing from a rebellion. Early painting in China was mostly wall-painting. Later, pictures were painted on paper or silk. The art reached its height in the Song dynasty and landscapes were the favourite subject. They were not pictures of places but general scenery, always showing mountains and water.

▲ This garden, called the 'Master of the Nets', can be seen today in eastern China. It was first laid out in the Song dynasty. Officials and educated people in China were very keen gardeners. Each garden was carefully designed with *pavilions*, lakes, bridges, trees and rocks. The gardens were supposed to reflect nature, the basic elements being rocks and water. Everything had a meaning, for example, water lilies stood for purity and truth.

INDUSTRY AND SCIENCE

The Chinese are a practical people and in ancient times they invented many things that made their lives easier. Several of the ideas were far in advance of those in the rest of the world at the time. They were particularly good at canal building and other methods of moving and using water. From the ground they extracted ores and used them to make metals. Their ideas about science, mathematics and *astronomy*, too, were well developed.

Coal was discovered early on in China. It helped in **smelting** iron ore which was used to make tools and weapons. The invention of **bellows**, often powered by water, and **furnaces** also made metal production much easier. Ores and salt were dug out of the ground from deep mines using methods unknown elsewhere in the world. The iron and salt industries became so valuable and the merchants so rich that the government took control of all production throughout China.

A doctor is curing a patient by burning ▶
special leaves over the part that hurts. This
method of healing is called moxibustion.
Moxibustion and acupuncture (which uses
needles to cure people) were often used in
ancient China. There were all kinds of herbal
remedies too and a large number of books
about medicine and illness were written.
Today people in the West are trying out these
age-old Chinese ways of healing people.

In the second century AD, the first ▼
earthquake detector was invented. When the
earth trembled, a ball would fall from one
dragon's mouth into one of the frogs' mouths.
Which one fell depended on the direction of
the quake. The principles of the compass too
were discovered in China at about the
same time. Other clever inventions
included the waterclock, the sundial
and the Chinese calculator called
the abacus. The abacus is
still used by school-
children all over
China today.

WAR AND DEFENCE

During the Warring States period, before China became one country, the Chinese developed all sorts of methods of warfare and weapons in order to fight each other. After China was united, wars were fought along the borders, particularly with tribes to the north. From the open grasslands that stretched in this direction, ferocious horsemen regularly swept down into China, killing and looting. The most successful were the Mongols, who conquered China in the thirteenth century.

▲ These lifesize model soldiers, known as the 'Terracotta Warriors', were built to guard the Qin emperor's tomb. Over 7,000 clay soldiers have been found buried in the earth – each one is different. They give us a good idea of an army in those days because the tomb had every kind of soldier (like bowmen and spearmen) as well as horses and chariots.

From Central Asia the Chinese bought fine strong horses, like the one in this Han dynasty bronze model, to help them in their wars against northern tribes. ▶ As for weapons, the most lethal in the early days was the crossbow. The bolt it fired could go much farther and with much more force than an arrow (it would have made great holes in Roman shields of the time). A revolution in weapons came with the use of gunpowder during the Song dynasty when bombs and mines were made and cannons and rocket launchers were used to fire missiles with poisonous gas.

◀ The Great Wall was built to protect China from the tribes to the north. Here there were no natural defences such as high mountains. The wall was first built by the Qin emperor and during following dynasties it was rebuilt and added to. It still stretches today for several thousand kilometres across northern China. Signals could be sent along the wall from watchtowers spaced along its length; in places it was wide enough for several horsemen to ride along together.

TRAVELLING

The Chinese empire was huge. By building new roads and improving their design, the Qin emperor made a great difference to the ease of travelling around. Road surfaces were better than anywhere else in the world at that time and bridges and ferries crossed the rivers. Messengers were able to travel quickly due to the relay system that had fresh horses ready for them at regular points along their journey.

Chariots like these ones shown on a Han dynasty tomb were used from early times in China. The rich could travel in carriages or on horseback but the poor usually walked. Wheelbarrows, carts and pack animals were used to carry goods around on land. The Chinese invented a good harness and stirrups that made the horse a very useful animal for both pulling loads and riding.

In this picture an ▶ emperor is going for a pleasure cruise on the Grand Canal. China's many rivers meant that boats were a good way of getting around. The two longest rivers, the Yellow and Yangzi Rivers, flowed from east to west. In order to link them so people and goods could travel north to south, a canal was built, stretching nearly 2,000 kilometres. Grain was paid like a tax to the government and the Grand Canal was particularly useful in bringing it to the capital.

◀ Another Chinese invention was a special kind of rudder, used to steer boats like these. It meant that the Chinese could sail very large boats. Even though they were able to build these, they never felt much need to explore beyond Chinese shores – only late in the Ming dynasty in AD 1405 did a fleet of ships set out to see the world. Before then, there was only one official exploration when, in 138 BC, Zhang Qian discovered Central Asia. He told the emperor of stories he had heard of another great empire to the west, the Roman Empire, but the two civilizations were never to meet.

TRADE

China was almost self-sufficient and needed little from other countries. Trade with distant countries probably began when the explorer Zhang Qian discovered fine horses in Central Asia, though jade had long been imported from neighbouring lands. Outsiders wanted to buy China's silk, iron and bronze and later china. An overland route called the Silk Road was used to make the journey to Central Asia. Later, when the route was blocked because of wars, Arab and Indian traders opened up sea routes to China.

The Silk Road once had many towns and cities along its route. This ruined city lies in one of the deserts of north-west China that had to be crossed by traders coming from Central Asia. Silk was sent to places as far away as Rome in Europe. Caravans would travel for months along these routes, often using camels on the desert stretches. During the Tang dynasty, China's capital Changan was crowded with foreign traders. The Tang emperors were the only ancient Chinese to be really interested in foreign ideas and people.

These ladies are ▶ pounding newly woven silk to make it softer before it is made into clothes. Silk has been made in China for at least 3,500 years. Silkworms feed on mulberry leaves and then weave *cocoons*. It is the thread from these cocoons that is spun to make the silk – one cocoon can have as much as one kilometre of thread on it. Silk was so important to China that silk making was a closely guarded secret, but two Persian monks managed to smuggle some silkworm eggs out in the sixth century.

Detail from *Court Ladies Preparing Newly Woven Silk*. Chinese and Japanese Special Fund; courtesy, Museum of Fine Arts, Boston.

▼ Ancient Chinese coins like these ones had holes in the middle. This meant that they could be carried on strings, sometimes in hundreds. The earliest currency was cowry shells, then miniature tools such as knives and spades were used. But the Qin emperor standardized the money so it could be used all over the country. The problem with metal coins was that large amounts were heavy to carry. When there was a shortage of metal in the Tang dynasty, paper money started to be used, the first of its kind in the world.

29

GLOSSARY

Ancestors   People's relations who lived before them.

Astronomy   The study of the stars and planets.

Bellows   An instrument for blowing air on to a fire to help it burn.

Buddhism   A religion that began in India in about 500 BC.

Ceremony   A formal act of doing something.

Civilization   A country or state with a high level of art, customs and laws.

Cocoons   A cocoon is the protective silk shell spun by a caterpillar before it becomes a butterfly or moth.

Droughts   Long periods without rain.

Dynasty   A line of rulers from the same family.

Fertile   Soil that produces good crops.

Furnace   A closed space like a room which is heated to a very high temperature.

Hemp   A plant with a strong stem that could be used to make things like ropes and clothes.

Imperial   To do with an empire or emperor.

Irrigation   Watering the land.

Jade   A precious stone, usually green, that the Chinese used to import.

Legend   A story passed down from generation to generation.

Millet   A kind of grain grown as a crop for food.

Pagoda   A tower with many levels.

Pavilions   Decorated buildings.

Peasants   People who work on the land, usually quite poor.

Philosophy   A way of understanding life.

Plough   A large metal tool which is dragged through a field to turn over the soil.

Population   The number of people who live in a country.

Rituals   Special ceremonies, usually religious.

Sacrifices   Making offerings to a god.

Scholars   Well-educated people.

Self-sufficient   Able to provide everything for oneself.

Smelting   Melting ores taken from the ground to produce metals.

Standardize   To make something regular and well ordered.

Tomb   A place where dead people are buried, usually underground.

Treadmill   A huge wheel that is turned by people climbing up its steps.

IMPORTANT DATES

The Chinese began to keep records about 3,000 years ago. Historians cannot be sure of exact dates before that time.

c 4500 BC   Farming settlements appear in the Yellow River valley

c 2200 – 1650 BC   China's first dynasty, the Xia

604 BC   Lao Zi supposed to have been born

551 BC   Confucius born

476 BC – 221 BC   Warring States period

221 BC Qin emperor unites China into one country

214 BC   Qin emperor instructs the building of the Great Wall

206 BC – AD 220   Han dynasty

138 BC   Zhang Qian travels to the west and discovers other civilizations and valuable horses

136 BC   Confucianism made the state religion

c AD 60   Buddhism arrives from India

c AD 105   Paper invented

c AD 130   Invention of the first earthquake detector

AD 610   Grand Canal completed linking Yellow and Yangzi Rivers

AD 618 – AD 907   Tang dynasty. The capital Changan the largest city in the world.

AD 700 – AD 800 Block printing invented and many more people able to read books

AD 960 – AD 1279   Song dynasty

AD 1271   Mongol armies of Kublai Khan invade China

AD 1368 – AD 1644   Ming dynasty

AD 1644 – AD 1911   Qing dynasty

PRONUNCIATION GUIDE

It may be helpful to remember the following when trying to pronounce Chinese words:
'zh' is said like 'j' in 'jumper'
'q' is said like 'ch' in 'chick'
'x' is said like 'sh' in 'shop'

BOOKS TO READ

The Ancient Chinese by Lai Po Kan (Macdonald, 1980)
This book uses artists' illustrations to show what Chinese life used to be like.

The Ancient World: The Chinese by Pamela Odijk (Heinemann Children's Reference, 1991)
A useful book covering most aspects of ancient China.

Ancient China by R. Nicholson and C. Watts (Franklin Watts, 1991)
This book mixes facts, stories and activities to give you an insight into the lives of the ancient Chinese.

INDEX